NIKOLA TESLA

A Life From Beginning to End

Copyright © 2017 by Hourly History

Table of Contents

Introduction

Early Life

Alternating Current and the Induction Motor

Patents, Radio and X-rays

Colorado Springs

Wardenclyffe Years

Personal Life

Later Years

Death

Tesla's Beliefs

10 Things You Never Knew About Nikola Tesla

Conclusion

Introduction

You love your smartphone. That goes without question. There are probably many other things in your life that you "love," too. Bet you couldn't get along without your refrigerator, oven or microwave. What about your electric lights? Don't you just hate it when the lights go out?

What happened to that alternating current? Since you're now sitting in the dark with only a lone candle to comfort you, you could think about how we came to have all of these modern conveniences.

They make life so convenient. So comfortable. Whom do we have to thank for that? Well, you could start with Nikola Tesla.

Tesla was many things in his life, but best known for his designs in modern alternating current, or AC. Power supplies and even our modern electrical grids wouldn't have been possible without him.

Nikola Tesla's life was a complicated one, and his brilliance would lead to a tortured existence. Tesla believed his mind to be superior to everyone else's - and he let others know it. Some of the smartest inventors of his time would work with him, but Tesla was already figuring out mathematical equations and complex scientific problems in his head.

Unfortunately, many of his inventions went no further than his head. So, take a look at what Nikola Tesla was all about. Relegated to virtual obscurity after his death in

1943, many of his projects have been gaining popular interest in the last twenty years.

You might say Nikola Tesla was an electrical genius. He certainly would qualify for a modern-day electrical engineer and physicist and would have loved the world of wireless connectivity we have today.

Tesla's brilliance would never be appreciated by the world in which he lived. He was creative in his own way, thinking about an idea, forming it fully in his mind, and then creating it for all the world to see. No one knows what Tesla's IQ score was, and no one should care; IQ is no longer looked on as the #1 magic bullet to a life of success. Many other factors are necessary in order to be someone who makes a difference during their lifetime.

Tesla relied on his imagination to fuel his life. More successful people come to mind when you think about who invented electricity or the radio. This could be because opportunities didn't always present themselves at opportune times to Nikola Tesla.

Whatever you know, or think you know, let's have a look at this marvel of a man whom some called brilliant, others called a "mad scientist," and everyone came to acknowledge as extremely necessary to life as we know it in the 21st century.

Chapter One

Early Life

"The present is theirs; the future for which I really worked, is mine."

—Nikola Tesla

Nikola Tesla was born in Europe, in modern-day Croatia, in the small village of Smiljian. Tesla was born on July 10, 1856. His father Milutin Tesla was an Eastern Orthodox priest and his mother Duka Tesla had an affinity for making home-crafted tools and appliances.

Tesla was the fourth of five children. He had an older brother Dane, and three sisters, Milka, Angelina, and Marica. When little Nikola was five years old, his brother Dane was killed in a horse-riding accident.

Although his mother never received any formal education, Tesla was sent to the primary school in Smiljian. There he began to learn arithmetic, religion, and German. When Tesla was seven, his family moved to the village of Gospic, where his father served the church there. Even when he was a child, Tesla loved to tinker with all kinds of machinery, and family and friends would marvel at his spectacular memory. Tesla always credited his photographic memory and his creative abilities to his mother's side of the family.

Nikola completed primary and middle school, and by 1870 he moved to Karlovac to attend school at the Higher Real Gymnasium. In Europe, a gymnasium is a type of school with a strong emphasis on academic learning. This type of secondary school was meant to prepare students for university life and advanced academic study.

From a very early age, Nikola Tesla could memorize entire books and mathematical tables that utterly befuddled those around him. He was able to learn new languages easily and never needed much sleep. During his time in school, Tesla discovered electricity through his physics professor. He knew nothing about it, only that he wanted to know more about this wonderful thing.

Because Tesla could perform integral calculus in his head, some of his teachers thought he was cheating. Tesla was able to complete four years of study in just three, graduating in 1873. After graduating, Tesla returned to Smiljian, where he contracted cholera. He was sick for nine months, and his family believed he would die. Tesla did recover, and in 1874 he ran away to the woods rather than be conscripted (drafted) into the Austro-Hungarian Army. During this time, he read many books and believed that his time in the outdoors made him stronger both physically and mentally.

In 1875 Tesla enrolled in Austrian Polytechnic in Graz, Austria, on a scholarship. During his first year there, he never missed a class, passed nine exams (twice as many as were required), and he quickly became one of the star students. In his second year, Tesla found himself at odds with one of his professors over perceived design flaws in the direct-current (DC) motors that were being demonstrated in class.

At this point in his life, Tesla worked from 3 a.m. to 11 p.m. every day, seven days a week, including Sundays and holidays. His professors believed he was working himself into an early grave, but Tesla continued on this schedule. At the end of his second year, Tesla lost his scholarship and became addicted to gambling. In his third year, he gambled away his allowance and his tuition money. He eventually did win back his initial losses and paid back his family.

Tesla did not graduate from the university, and he received no grades for his third year. By 1878, Tesla left the university and cut all ties with his family. He did not want them to know he had dropped out of school. He worked as a draftsman in Slovenia for a while and continued gambling.

At this time, Tesla's father Milutin came to him, begging him to come home. Tesla refused, suffering a nervous breakdown. The following year, 1879, Tesla's father died from an unknown illness. Some say he suffered a stroke. Tesla returned to his high school, the Real Gymnasium, where he taught a large class of students.

In 1880, two of Tesla's uncles saved up enough money for him to leave for Prague and study at Charles-Ferdinand University. He arrived there too late to enroll; he didn't know Greek, which was a required subject; and he couldn't write in Czech. He did attend some classes, which he attended as an auditor, which meant he did not receive grades for them.

In 1881 Tesla moved to Budapest, Hungary. There he worked for the Budapest Telephone Exchange. While walking through a park one day with a friend, Tesla had a vision, and he quickly drew a diagram in the dirt to demonstrate for his friend a motor using the principle of rotating magnetic fields created by two or more alternating currents. There were no motors run on alternating current at the time, and there wouldn't be until Tesla came up with the idea of the induction motor several years later.

While in Budapest, Tesla developed a sketch for a rotating magnetic field – an idea which is still today used in many electromechanical devices. This would be the foundation from which many of his future inventions would spring.

In 1882, Tesla moved to France and continued making improvements to electrical equipment, but no one showed any particular interest in his ideas. In June 1884 Tesla immigrated to New York City with only four cents in his pocket. Immediately Tesla was hired by Thomas Edison to work at his Edison Machine Works on the Lower East Side of Manhattan.

Tesla had only met with Edison a few times. One of those times was when he stayed up all night repairing damaged dynamos on the ocean liner SS Oregon. On returning home early in the morning, he ran into Edison, who assumed he had been out all night having a good time. Tesla informed Edison he had been out all night, but working to fix a major problem. Edison was impressed.

Tesla went from solving simpler electrical engineering problems for Edison to involving himself in more complicated electrical problems. When he was hired, Tesla claims that Edison had offered him $50,000 to improve upon the DC (direct-current) generation plants that Edison looked on so favorably.

Edison had a reputation for being stingy with money, and everyone who knew him knew he did not have that kind of money available. Tesla went to work on improving Edison's generators and, when finished, asked Edison for payment.

Edison refused to pay up. He is quoted as saying, "when you become a full-fledged American, you will appreciate an American joke." Tesla was offered a $10-a-week raise over his $18-a-week salary. Tesla immediately quit.

Chapter Two

Alternating Current and the Induction Motor

"If Edison had a needle to find in a haystack, he would proceed at once with the diligence of the bee to examine straw after straw until he found the object of his search. I was a sorry witness of such doing that a little theory and calculation would have saved him ninety percent of his labor."

—Nikola Tesla

All throughout history, even after the invention of such culture-changing things as the printing press and more improved methods of plowing, electricity remained that elusive inspiration. Oh, it had been hinted at by men such as Benjamin Franklin, when in 1752 Franklin tied a metal key to the end of a damp kite string and flew a kite in a thunderstorm. Sparks began flying from the key to the back of Franklin's hand, proving to him that lightning was very much an electrical force.

As the nineteenth century was coming into its final decades, people still lit their homes with candles and oil lamps. The world was just waiting for someone to harness the power of electricity and make it work for everyone.

If there was one thing Nikola Tesla was sure of, it was his superior mind. No one else came close. After his time with Edison came to an end, Tesla partnered with two businessmen, Robert Lane and Benjamin Vail, and Tesla Electric Light & Manufacturing was created in 1886. The first patents issued to Tesla were for dynamo electric machine commutators, and it was these that were installed along with electrical arc light based illumination systems.

This dynamo machine helped reduce sparking, which was very common in electrical commutators of the day. Tesla had many ideas for new motors and electric transmission equipment, but his investors were not interested. In time, Tesla was left with no more money for his electric company. He also lost control of the patents he had created.

In the winter of 1886/1887, Tesla was digging ditches for $2/day to make money. Even he felt that all his higher education had been for nothing. Late in 1886. Tesla went to work for the Western Union Company. Along with Charles Peck, a New York attorney, and Alfred Brown, a Western Union superintendent, the Tesla Electric Company was created in April 1887.

Tesla, Brown, and Peck set up a laboratory in downtown Manhattan on Liberty Street, where Tesla was at last able to work on his electric motors, generators, and other devices. Not far from Edison's offices in NYC, Tesla was testing AC power systems that are still used around the world today.

The AC induction motor which Tesla built ran on alternating current. This was a power system which was taking hold in Europe and the United States because it offered advantages of being able to run high-voltage transmission lines over long distances.

The motor used polyphase current, which generated a rotating magnetic field that turned the motor. This induction motor was patented in May 1888. It was a simple self-starting motor which did not need a commutator, which meant there was no sparking.

Also in 1888, the editor of Electrical World magazine made it possible for Tesla to demonstrate his alternating current system. Engineers working for the Westinghouse Company reported back to their boss George Westinghouse that Nikola Tesla looked like he was really onto something with his AC motor. This was something for which Westinghouse was trying to secure patents.

Westinghouse did have his own induction motor ready to go, but he concluded that Tesla's would probably be vastly popular over his own. So, later in 1888, Brown and Peck negotiated a licensing deal with George Westinghouse for Tesla's Polyphase Induction Motor. Sixty thousand dollars in cash and stock and a royalty of $2.50 per AC horsepower produced by each motor was what they came up with.

Westinghouse also hired Tesla to be a consultant for the Westinghouse Company for $2,000 per month. While working for Westinghouse, Tesla moved to Pittsburgh, Pennsylvania where he worked on developing alternating current to power the city's streetcars.

By this time, because Tesla was working for Westinghouse, he and his AC induction motor and the licensing of the patent put him in direct competition with Thomas Edison. An electrical distribution battle known as the "War of Currents" soon began. This began because Westinghouse held the patent for his own AC system to power arc lights and incandescent lamps and Edison held all of the patents for DC lighting and the incandescent lightbulb.

Because Tesla's AC induction motor design was on Westinghouse's side, the company was on its way to building a completed integrated AC system. The costs of litigation and of hiring the best engineers meant that Tesla's motor had to be put on hold for the time being.

By 1890, Edison Machine Works was pursuing AC development. Two years later, with Thomas Edison no longer in control of his company, it was consolidated into a conglomerate called General Electric and was converting all of its systems to AC power.

At the beginning of 1893, engineers at Westinghouse had made great strides in developing the best version of Tesla's induction motor to date. At this point, Westinghouse Electric began branding their complete Polyphase AC system the "Tesla Polyphase System." Tesla's patents surely gave them priority over any other AC patents.

Much to the dismay of Thomas Edison, Westinghouse won the bid that lit the 1893 World's Columbian Exposition in Chicago with alternating current. They bid one million dollars more than General Electric. At this

World's Fair, there was an entire building devoted to electrical exhibits.

This was key to introducing the reliability, power, and safety of electricity into everyday life in America. Using the banner of the "Tesla Polyphase System," Tesla demonstrated a series of electrical effects; many of which had already been performed all over Europe and the U.S.

One of the experiments went like this: inside a room, there were two hard-rubber plates covered with tin foil and suspended in the air. These were about fifteen feet apart from each other and served as terminals for the wires leading from the transformers. Laying on a table in-between the two suspended plates, with no wires connected to them, were lamps or tubes. When the current was turned on these lamps or tubes glowed. Anyone in the room could have also held these lamps in their hand with the same effect.

Despite all this notoriety, the Westinghouse Company would have been in dire financial straits if George Westinghouse hadn't begged Tesla to forego the royalties they had once agreed upon. Tesla, who was very grateful to the man who had believed in him and his inventions, tore up the royalty contract.

In doing so, Tesla walked away from becoming one of the wealthiest men of the Gilded Age. He could have become a multi-millionaire, the likes of John D. Rockefeller, John Jacob Astor, J.P. Morgan, and Andrew Carnegie. He walked away from millions in royalties that were due him and billions more that would have come his way over time.

Maybe he felt thankful to be in America. In July 1891, at age 35, Tesla became a naturalized citizen of the United States. He established a laboratory on South Fifth Avenue in Manhattan and another one on E. Houston Street. At both of these locations, he lit electric lamps wirelessly. He also patented his Tesla coil.

The Tesla coil laid the foundation for the development of wireless technologies and is still used today in radio technology. The next time you pick up your cell phone, remember to thank Nikola Tesla.

Chapter Three

Patents, Radio and X-rays

"Many people die at 25 and aren't buried until 75."

—Benjamin Franklin

Creativity seemed to blossom in the last half of the nineteenth century all over the world. Suddenly, there were numerous inventions that were springing up all over the place. Everything from Coca-Cola to the elevator, kindergarten to cotton candy, from dynamite to potato chips, typewriters, vacuum cleaners, hot dogs, zippers, radio, x-rays, and lots more, there wasn't any aspect of life that wasn't looking positively modern.

By the 1890s, electricity was one of the major inventions that were just getting started. From the lowly light bulb, there would arise an entire industry that was waiting to encompass the world. Nikola Tesla was a huge part of this brand-new effort.

In 1893, the man who headed up the Niagara Falls Cataract Construction Company, Edward Dean Adams, sought out Tesla's help in figuring out the best option for producing electric power at the Falls. Up to this point, there had been competitions and other proposals on the best way to capture the dynamism of water.

Among the systems already proposed were ideas around two-phase and three-phase AC, high-voltage DC, and compressed air. Adams was looking for the best selection, and he turned to Tesla for the best advice. Tesla advised him that a two-phase system would work the best and that at Westinghouse there was already a two-phase system in place to light incandescent bulbs using alternating current.

Adams' construction company awarded a contract to Westinghouse Electric to build a two-phase system at Niagara Falls. Because Westinghouse had already demonstrated how an AC system works at the Colombian Exposition and Tesla had advised this would be most successful, the Niagara Falls Construction Company decided on Westinghouse to do the job.

However, they also awarded another contract to General Electric to build the AC distribution system. By the mid-1890s, General Electric, which was backed by financier J.P. Morgan, was involved in patent battles and attempting to take over Westinghouse Electric. By 1896 a patent sharing agreement was created between GE and Westinghouse. Also in this year, the city of Buffalo, New York was lit up using the power of the Niagara Falls. This accomplishment was heard about all around the world.

The alternating current system of electricity quickly became the first-rate power system that would be used in the 20th century. It has remained the worldwide standard ever since the 1890s.

Westinghouse continued to struggle financially. Just like today, when companies fall on hard times, they tend to look at things they've supported in the past. If they feel it isn't worth it, they let it go.

A similar thing happened to Tesla's patent. The bankers for Westinghouse Electric felt that this patent was causing a real strain on the company. George Westinghouse had already paid out $200,000 to Tesla, Brown, and Peck in licenses and royalties. This was a phenomenal amount of money for the times.

By 1897, Westinghouse advised Tesla that he would no longer be able to pay out royalties as he had in the past, and there was a possibility that he would lose control of his company. If that happened, Tesla would have to deal with the bankers for his royalties.

Westinghouse convinced Tesla to release the company from the licensing agreement over the AC patents. Instead, Westinghouse Electric purchased the AC patents outright for $216,000. This kind of a deal would never be made in today's competitive business atmosphere; in the late nineteenth century, it seemed to have its allure.

For Tesla, this was a dream come true. With the money he had made from his patents, he was able to pursue his own dreams. He now had the time and the money to set up his own shop. In 1889, Tesla moved out of the Liberty Street shop that he shared with Brown and Peck.

For the next twelve years, Tesla worked out of his workshops and laboratories in Manhattan. These included one on Grand Street, the fourth floor of a building on South Fifth Avenue, and the sixth and seventh floors of a building on East Houston Street. It would be in these places that Tesla and his staff would conduct some of their best magic.

If you remember the movie Frankenstein, where the electricity seems to travel down a large coil to the poor cadaver laying on the table, this movie device actually looks very much like the Tesla coil.

Tesla invented his electrical resonant transformer circuit in 1891 as a power supply for what he called his "System of Electric Lighting." This coil produces high-voltage, low-current, high-frequency alternating-current electricity.

Two years earlier, Tesla had traveled to Paris to visit the 1889 Exposition Universelle. There he learned about radio waves. Tesla decided to explore this more deeply. He experimented with different materials before settling on a coil which had an air gap instead of insulating material, which was forever over-heating.

This Tesla coil was capable of generating high voltages and frequencies, which led to new forms of light, such as fluorescent and neon, as well as x-rays. By conducting many experiments, he and his team were able to ascertain that the Tesla coil made it possible to send and receive radio signals. In 1897, Tesla applied for American patents, beating out the Italian inventor Marconi for the rights.

Beginning in the mid-1890s, Tesla began experimenting on what he called "invisible" energy, after taking notice of damaged film from old experiments. His first experiments were with electrical discharge tubes. Even before Wilhelm Rontgen's discovery of x-rays, Tesla may have inadvertently captured an x-ray image.

Once Rontgen's x-ray imagery was known, Tesla kept experimenting and eventually came up with a single terminal vacuum tube that worked in conjunction with the Tesla coil. Decades later, Tesla recalled how experimenting with this vacuum tube caused a stinging pain, very sharp as it entered his body, and another pain where the x-ray passed out of his body. He suffered skin damage when experimenting with his new x-ray technology.

One of the most intriguing of all of Tesla's experiments was with wireless technology that he started working on in the 1890s. He was fascinated with the idea that electrical power could be transmitted without the use of wires, many decades before it actually became popular in culture.

Because Tesla was already using coils to transmit power in wireless lighting experiments, he believed it was entirely possible to see all electrical power done wirelessly. Tesla knew that wireless power would transmit large amounts of power all around the globe, and he realized that worldwide communication would be just as feasible. His ideas about wireless technology were certainly attainable in his mind; at the time, there was no real way to see them work.

Chapter Four

Colorado Springs

"The successful person makes a habit of doing what the failing person doesn't like to do."

—Thomas Edison

The above quote applies to every inventor who ever lived and will live. Nothing is ever created that doesn't go through a thousand tries and numerous failings. The spark of an idea is what sees these people through; they are determined to make it happen. Then, when they fail again, they go right on trying.

In 1898 Tesla came up with a radio-controlled boat, which he demonstrated to the crowds at an exhibition in Madison Square Garden in New York City. Tesla tried to sell this idea to the U.S. Military; something which could be developed as a radio-controlled torpedo, but none of them was interested.

It wouldn't be until World War I and beyond, that remote control radio would begin to catch on. That didn't deter Tesla. He continued talking about what he called "Teleautomatics," even addressing a meeting in Chicago while he was on his way to Colorado Springs in May 1899.

It was at this time that Tesla moved his laboratory to Colorado Springs, where he could conduct his high-frequency, high voltage experiments. His lab was on the corner of Foote Ave. and Kiowa St. and Tesla had friends there who would supply him with all of the power he would need to conduct further experiments.

The polyphase alternating current power distribution system was already in place in Colorado Springs, and Tesla told reporters that he planned on conducting wireless telegraphy experiments and that his wireless signals would stretch all the way from Pike's Peak to Paris, France.

As the nineteenth century rolled into the twentieth, Tesla was busy in Colorado Springs, conducting his electrical experiments. His first experiment in June 1899 produced a spark of only five inches in length that was both very noisy and thick. Tesla took his time observing atmospheric electricity or lightning storms. He came away with a firm resolution that the Earth had something called resonant frequency.

Resonant frequencies are the natural frequencies at which it is easiest to get an object to vibrate. Most objects have more than one resonant frequency. Musical instruments, for instance, have positive resonant frequencies, whereas bridges have negative resonant frequencies.

Everything has a natural frequency. This is referred to as normal mode. You can't "resonate" an object. However, you can use various waves (mechanical, electromagnetic) at its natural frequency to build up gigantic amplitudes.

Tesla was able to produce artificial lightning consisting of millions of volts and up to 135 feet long.

While conducting his many experiments in the lab at Colorado Springs, Tesla observed unusual signals from his receiver, which he thought may be coming from another planet. Reports were immediately noted over the story, and reporters erroneously wrote that Tesla was receiving radio signals from Mars.

At the same time, Tesla was conducting his experiments, Marconi was conducting his own European experiments. In a naval demonstration, Marconi may have transmitted the letter "S," which would have sounded like dot/dot/dot. This may have been what Tesla was picking up. Or some other wireless transmitter could have been sending signals.

In 1899, the American businessman John Jacob Astor IV invested $100,000 so that Tesla could further develop and create a new lighting system. Astor would lose his life aboard the ocean liner Titanic in 1912. Tesla used the money to further his experiments at his Colorado Springs lab.

In January 1900, Tesla made one last entry in his journal for his lab experiments. Four years later the lab at Colorado Springs was torn down, and everything inside was sold to pay his debts.

Had Tesla never conducted his wireless experiments in Colorado Springs, he would never have prepared himself for establishing the trans-Atlantic wireless telecommunications facility which went by the name of Wardenclyffe near Shoreham, Long Island.

Tesla was granted new patents for "a system of transmitting electrical energy" and "an electrical transmitter." When Marconi made his first trans-Atlantic radio transmission the following year, Tesla bragged that it was done with 17 Tesla patents, though it was never proved to be so.

Tesla's years in Colorado Springs were productive ones, and, for Tesla, brought him ever closer to inventing wireless communications for the entire world. It was here that he developed what he thought was his most important discovery – terrestrial stationary waves. Tesla proved that the Earth could be used as a conductor and could be considered a giant tuning fork to electrical vibrations that were sent out at certain frequencies.

It was in Colorado Springs that Tesla created man-made lighting. He even lit 200 lamps, all without wires, from 25 miles away.

Chapter Five

Wardenclyffe Years

"I am even grateful to Einstein and others because through their erroneous theories they lead mankind away from that dangerous path I followed."

—Nikola Tesla

In 1900 with $150,000 in loan money (over $4M in today's money) from J.P. Morgan, Tesla began construction of his Wardenclyffe Tower in Shoreham, Long Island, which lies approximately 100 miles east of New York City. Unfortunately, Tesla would run out of money before the tower was even finished. So, again he appealed to Morgan for more money, but Morgan felt Tesla had breached his contract by not using previous monies for specified projects. He refused to lend Tesla any more money.

In 1901 Marconi successfully sent a signal from England to Newfoundland. Tesla had complained that it was done using his patents, but courts decided in Marconi's favor. The U. S. Supreme Court eventually did uphold Tesla's claims, but not until 1943, after his death.

Marconi would be the one to go on as the man who invented the radio and would become very wealthy for having done so. With the backing of Thomas Edison and

Andrew Carnegie, Marconi would continue making great advances in radio technology.

However, it had been Nikola Tesla who, in 1897, had applied for two patents, US645576 and US649621, for radio technology. It was thought that the courts sided with Marconi because of two extremely famous and wealthy backers. The U.S. Government would avoid paying Tesla any royalties as well.

The heart of radio transmission is based on four tuned circuits, which are used for transmitting radio waves and receiving them. This is Tesla's original concept, not Marconi's. In 1893, at the Franklin Institute in Philadelphia, Tesla had demonstrated this concept during a lecture there. Tesla's four circuits are still what is used today in all television and radio equipment.

Over the next five years, Tesla would write Morgan over 50 letters pleading for more money. Tesla had been facing foreclosure even before he started building his tower. In 1902 the tower was finally erected and stood 186 feet tall. In June of that year, Tesla moved his entire operations from Manhattan to Wardenclyffe Tower.

The following year, in yet another letter to Morgan, Tesla explained that besides just wireless communication, Wardenclyffe Tower would also be capable of wireless transmission of electric power. Morgan finally replied that he could no longer have anything to do with this matter.

Wardenclyffe was sold for $20,000 and in 1917 was torn down to make way for more valuable real estate. This defeat, which Tesla claimed to be his worst, led to another of his breakdowns. He knew his experiments cost money to finance, and he couldn't understand why those with money wouldn't back him up. He couldn't understand "a faint-hearted, doubting world!"

So, what was Tesla to do now? He believed the one area he could successfully navigate would be that of the consultant; so that's what he did. However, his ideas would prove too outlandish, and his eccentricities were beginning to take over his life.

Chapter Six

Personal Life

"Seldom did one meet a scientist or engineer, who was also a poet, a philosopher, an appreciator of fine music, a linguist, and a connoisseur of fine food and drink."

– Julian Hawthorne

Nikola Tesla never married. At 6 feet 2 inches tall, he was always a stylish, elegant man, and his weight stayed the same all through his life. He was a well-groomed gentleman and very disciplined in his daily life.

There was a thorough description given about him by Arthur Brisbane, who was a newspaper editor for the New York World:

"Nikola Tesla is almost the tallest, almost the thinnest and certainly the most serious man who goes to Delmonico's regularly . . . He has eyes set very far back in his head. They are rather light. I asked him how he could have such light eyes and be a Slav. He told me that his eyes were once much darker, but that using his mind a great deal had made them many shades lighter. I have often heard it said that using the brain makes the eyes lighter in color. Tesla's confirmation of the theory through his personal experience is important.

He is very thin, is more than six feet tall and weighs less than a hundred and forty pounds. He has very big hands. Many able men do – Lincoln is one instance. His thumbs are remarkably big, even for such big hands. They are extraordinarily big. This is a good sign. The thumb is the intellectual part of the hand. The apes have very small thumbs. Study them, and you will notice this.

Nikola Tesla has a head that spreads out at the top like a fan. His head is shaped like a wedge. His chin is as pointed as an icepick. His mouth is too small. His chin, though not weak, is not strong enough. His face cannot be studied and judged like the faces of other men, for he is not a worker in practical fields. He lives his life up in the top of his head, where ideas are born, and up there he has plenty of room. His hair is jet black and curly. He stoops – most men do when they have no peacock blood in them. He lives inside of himself. He takes a profound interest in his own work. He has that supply of self-love and self-confidence which usually goes with success. And he differs from most men who are written and talked about in the fact that he has something to tell."

Tesla attributed his scientific abilities to his chastity. In his early years, Tesla believed women to be superior to men. That started to change when he began witnessing the many areas that women were starting to involve themselves in as the nineteenth century gave way to the twentieth.

Tesla believed women were trying to compete with men and in so doing, were losing all of their feminine ways. In an interview with the Galveston Daily News in

August 1924, Tesla is quoted as saying "In place of the soft-voiced, gentle woman of my reverent worship, has come the woman who thinks that her chief success in life lies in making herself as much as possible like man – in dress, voice and actions, in sports and achievements of every kind . . . The tendency of woman to push aside man, supplanting the old spirit of cooperation with him in all the affairs of life, is very disappointing to me."

Tesla always believed all the stimulation in life he needed was to be found in his workshops and laboratories. He avoided social situations, preferring to remain asocial. He loved secluding himself in his work. Those who did know him, though, always spoke highly of him, as one who was very sincere and sweet.

Even though Tesla was asocial and avoided being with people, he did so because he felt this was the only way to further his work. You could say he was the ultimate geek. Tesla was a handsome man who knew quite a few ladies but refused to date, stating that relationships were sure to get in the way of his calling: being the inventor he knew himself to be.

And what do geeks do best? Why, they stay up all night long, taking something apart, only to put it all back together again. They tinker with things that aren't broken and visualize new ways of using them. They really are not too concerned with the world they are living in because they are too busy inventing a new world.

You could say that Nikola Tesla was the ultimate mad scientist, and you would be right. His inventions stand on their own and still are used in the world we live in today.

Chapter Seven

Later Years

"Everything is energy and that's all there is to it. Match the frequency of the reality you want and you cannot help but get that reality. It can be no other way. This is not philosophy. This is physics."

—Albert Einstein

In 1906, Tesla turned 50 years old. It was on his birthday that he demonstrated a bladeless 200-horsepower turbine engine. His bladeless turbine engines would continue to be tested at speeds of between 50 to 1,000 horsepower by 1910-11.

Still living near bankruptcy during these years, Tesla sued the Marconi Company in 1915 for infringement of his wireless tuning patents. Twelve years previously his patents had been upheld by the courts; the decision had been reversed in 1904. It wouldn't be until 1943 that the U. S. Supreme Court would find in favor of Oliver Lodge, John Stone, and Tesla over patents that Marconi had sued the US government over. Because Marconi's claim to certain patents was questionable, he had no right to claim infringement on those same claims.

In 1912 Tesla believed that applying electricity to the brain would make students smarter. He wanted to wire the rooms of classes with electric waves which would vibrate at high frequencies. The plan was actually approved by the superintendent of schools in New York but never implemented.

Before the start of World War I in 1914, Tesla was still seeking investors overseas. Once the war started, he lost all funding from European countries. However, in 1917 he did receive the American Institute of Electrical Engineers' highest honor, the Edison Medal.

By 1917, Tesla believed that electricity could be used to find submarines. This would be made possible by the reflection of an electric ray at high-frequency viewed on a fluorescent screen. He was not correct in believing that high-frequency waves would penetrate water. Years later, it would be shown that his dreaming about high-frequency signals was correct.

Tesla had no way of proving his ideas, and many of his visions and prophecies stayed in his head. Yet, when he dreamed, according to Emile Girardeau, who helped develop France's first radar system in the 1930s, Tesla dreamed correctly.

After the First World War had ended, Tesla spent the next five years working in Milwaukee, Wisconsin for the company Allis-Chalmers. Here he spent most of his time working with the chief engineer. They were an American manufacturing company and the railway and lighting division of the Westinghouse Company. It was here they tried perfecting Tesla's turbine engine.

TIME Magazine featured Tesla on the cover when Tesla was 75 years old in 1931. Later in the year, Tesla announced that he was on the verge of discovering a brand new type of energy. What it was and where it would come from would be from an entirely new and different source.

By 1934 Tesla was once again working for the Westinghouse Company. He was paid $125 a month, plus his rent at the New Yorker Hotel was paid by the company. Westinghouse may have been worried about any bad publicity he would receive on how poorly he had treated Tesla years ago. Because Tesla would not accept charity, Westinghouse used the paying of his hotel room as his consulting fee.

Their star inventor was now a nearly impoverished man, and a very obsessive-compulsive one, too. Tesla became obsessed with cleanliness and also with the number three. He would shake hands with people and then wash his hands, all done in sets of three. He always counted his steps whenever he walked and always had to have 18 napkins on the table at all times when eating.

In 1935 Tesla was approached by the Pierce-Arrow auto manufacturer and also George Westinghouse to develop an electric motor that would power a car. The motor Tesla produced was small, and was approximately 80 horsepower. The engine, which was a small, 12-volt storage battery, was connected to the dashboard with two thick wires.

Tesla then connected the wires to a small black box which he made out of materials bought in a local radio store. With his little black box, Tesla was able to test the car for over a week, at speeds of up to 90 mph. No one was allowed to inspect the black box and could only take Tesla's word for it that the energy produced by it was "a mysterious radiation that came out of the aether."

When news of Tesla and his little black box became public, many thought he was losing his mind. There were those who claimed Tesla was in cahoots with alien forces in the universe and at the very least he was practicing black magic. Either way, he and his black box were anything but popular, so Tesla did what he always did; took his equipment back to New York City and spoke about it no more.

As time went by, one of the things Tesla loved to do was to go out into the city and feed the pigeons. In the fall of 1937, some time after midnight, Tesla went out for a walk and to feed his beloved pigeons. While crossing a street a few blocks from his hotel, he couldn't get out of the way of a taxicab quick enough and was thrown heavily to the ground.

Some of his ribs were broken, and his back was severely injured, but Tesla refused to see a doctor, something he had avoided all his life. All he asked was to be taken home where he remained, in bed, for some months to come. Finally, in 1938, he was able to get around, but his pigeons had disappeared from his window. He resumed taking walks to feed the pigeons and even had someone else go for him when he wasn't up to it.

One of Tesla's most intriguing inventions was something called a teleforce weapon, or death ray. Tesla believed it could be used against ground troops or for anti-aircraft purposes. Tesla said his apparatus would send concentrated beams of particles through the free air with such tremendous energy that it would have the ability to bring down a fleet of 10,000 enemy airplanes at a distance of 200 miles. Armies, he said, would drop dead in their tracks.

In 1934, the New York Times had run a headline that screamed, "TESLA AT 78, BARES NEW 'DEATH BEAM'", and went on to describe how this new teleforce invention produced massive amounts of energy that could be used to stop armies. Tesla was criticized as just another "mad scientist," but he never let others stop him from turning his imagination to reality.

Tesla claimed to have worked on this death ray technology from about 1900 until his death in 1943. At a luncheon in his honor in 1937, Tesla reflected that he had built, demonstrated, and used his death ray machine. "Only a little time will pass before I give it to the world."

The death ray device was based on a narrow stream of pellets made of tungsten that would be charged via high voltage. Tesla had also written a treatise all about charged particle beam weapons. He wanted to describe a superweapon that would put an end to all war.

His teleforce weapon is described as an open-ended vacuum tube with a gas jet seal that allows particles to escape. There was also a method of charging particles to millions of volts and another method of creating and directing the particle streams. Tesla wanted very much for the governments of the U.S., the U.K., the Soviet Union, and Yugoslavia to show interest in his death ray.

While negotiations with these governments were going on, Tesla revealed that someone had tried to steal his invention. His room had been entered and all of his papers closely looked at, but there was no blueprint to find. Tesla, as he did with most everything he invented, had the blueprint locked safely away in his mind, where no one could get at it.

Upon his death, the FBI had all of Tesla's belongings seized, even though he was an American citizen. Everything was thoroughly scrutinized by one John G. Trump, uncle of Donald J. Trump, 45th president of the United States. The public was told that there were rumors that Tesla had invented a death ray and the government didn't want the information to pass into enemy hands.

For 73 years, that's how it stayed. Thanks to the Freedom of Information Act, Tesla's papers were declassified, and now it can be revealed that the FBI documents prove Tesla's Death Ray was not something merely invented by the overactive minds of science fiction authors.

The FBI knew that, during his lifetime, Tesla had conducted many experiments in connection with the wireless transmission of electrical power, and that the U.S. government had been very interested in his "death ray" technology. What they would have done with it, or what they have done with it, is anybody's guess, but if you are interested in those classified documents, they are available to you.

Chapter Eight

Death

"The world will wait a long time for Nikola Tesla's equal in achievement and imagination."

—E. Armstrong

Destitute and bankrupt at the end of his life, Tesla became obsessed with pigeons. While living at the New Yorker Hotel, he claims that one female white pigeon used to visit his window ledge with great regularity. At one point this white pigeon appeared and flew in his window. Tesla believed she was there to let him know she was dying. He claims to have seen two powerful, intense beams of light coming from the eyes of the pigeon; the light that was more dazzling than anything he had seen in his laboratory. The pigeon died in his arms, and Tesla knew that he too, had come to the end of his earthly life.

On January 7, 1943, right in the middle of World War II, Tesla died alone in his room of the New Yorker hotel. His body was not discovered for two days until a maid ignoring his "Do Not Disturb" sign on the door opened it. It seems Tesla died from a heart attack.

Immediately, the FBI seized all of Tesla's belongings, even though he was an American citizen. John Trump, a professor at M.I.T., was called in to analyze everything.

He concluded that there was nothing there that would be considered dangerous if it fell into enemy hands. There were those who believed Tesla had concocted a "death ray" machine; all Trump found was an old box called a decade box, which was a type of test equipment.

On January 12, over two thousand people attended the funeral for Tesla held at the Cathedral of St. John the Divine. His remains were cremated. In 1952, all of Tesla's belongings and his ashes were shipped to Belgrade, Serbia. If you ever visit the Nikola Tesla Museum there, you can see Tesla's ashes in a gold-plated sphere displayed on a marble pedestal. The entire museum underwent a reconstruction in 2006. Here you can learn all about Tesla's many inventions, including his famous Tesla coil, his Polyphase System, a two-phase induction motor, and even his baptismal certificate.

Chapter Nine

Tesla's Beliefs

"Thousands of geniuses live and die undiscovered – either by themselves or by others."

—Mark Twain

It seems Tesla never let a minute of his life go by without being busy in it. Between never marrying nor having a family, not sleeping very much and not being one for seeking people out socially, all of his passions were thrown into his work. That doesn't mean he lived in a vacuum.

Up until the 20th century, scientists, and people in general, believed in an "ether" that covered the atmosphere, and this is where energy, including electricity, came from. Because Tesla held this belief, his writings reflected a pre-atomic mindset. Tesla couldn't understand that there was such a thing as subatomic particles.

Tesla questioned the existence of electrons and felt that if they existed at all they were in some alternate state of matter, could only exist in a vacuum, and had nothing to do with electricity. He also believed atoms were what they were; that they had no ability to change in any way. They could not change or split.

Tesla questioned Einstein's theory of relativity. He is quoted as saying about this theory that "I hold that space cannot be curved, for the simple reason that it can have no properties. It might be said that God has properties. He has not, but only attributes, and these are of our own making. Of properties we can only speak when dealing with matter filling the space. To say that in the presence of large bodies space becomes curved is equivalent to stating that something can act upon nothing. I, for one, refuse to subscribe to such a view."

Tesla didn't subscribe to such a view because he had already developed his own theory regarding matter and energy that he had been working on since 1882. When he was 81 years old, Tesla announced he had completed a dynamic theory of gravity. He claimed he had it all worked out, and it was only a matter of time before he gave it to the world. Unfortunately, nothing was ever found in his papers that hinted of this dynamic theory of gravity.

Tesla, like many who grew up in the 19th century, believed in a selective breeding version of eugenics. He didn't so much believe that there should be a "master race," but that because humans had taken "pity" on others over the centuries, this had resulted in the stopping of the natural workings of nature.

Tesla believed that the "unfit" should be sterilized so they could no longer continue breeding. He was in agreement with other eugenicists, who wanted to make marriage more difficult to attain. They believed that certain people, who were unfit to be parents, should never become parents. Tesla believed in the decades to come that people would have a clear sense of who they were marrying and would stay away from those undesirables, just like they would from violent criminals.

Tesla was well aware that women were beginning to have their voices heard and that gender equality was something many of them were working toward. Humanity's future, Tesla believed, would be run by "Queen Bees." Women would eventually make their way into higher education and executive levels of business and industry, and that the future would be run by women.

Tesla's philosophy was of the humanist kind. Everyone had the ability to improve his or her life through education and reason and imagination and did not have to submit to a State or government which threw authority or tradition in your face. Such a body of government like the League of Nations, which would become the United Nations, would never solve the problems of nations worldwide.

Tesla had been raised in the Eastern Orthodox Church while he was growing up in Serbia, but later in his life, he did not believe in any organized religion. He also very much opposed anyone who bordered on a religious fanatic stance. He loved reading all about Christianity and Buddhism.

Early on, Tesla seemed to agree with ancient teachings where the teachings of religion helped to bring about peace and harmony. The "we are all one" philosophy was the one he had the most respect for, yet just a few years before World War II would start Tesla stated that it was science which reigned because it was founded on fact. Over time and centuries, mechanisms had come along which were extremely complex, but as far as a "soul" or "spirit" was concerned, this was nothing more than what made up each person's body. When that body ceased to function, so did the soul.

Tesla did write a number of books and articles. My Inventions: The Autobiography of Nikola Tesla, as well as most of his writings, are available free or for little money from the internet.

Tesla's legacy does live on. Besides being honored on the cover of TIME Magazine when he was 75 years old, Tesla has been the subject of numerous TV, films, live theater, books, and even video games. Over his lifetime, he received over 70 congratulatory letters from esteemed scientists and pioneers, including Albert Einstein.

For a scientist who never achieved the wealth and status of others like Einstein or Edison, Tesla was one of the most celebrated personalities in the press in the 20th century. When Life Magazine published a special issue in September 1997, he was recognized as one of the most famous 100 people of the last 1,000 years.

Even though Tesla's writings found their way into scientific journals and literary and intellectual publications of the day, he never seemed to be the one people pointed to when they thought about famous inventors. However, it was his discoveries, his inventions, and most of all, his vision, which made so many other things possible. Who knows how many young people he inspired by all he accomplished?

Tesla was inducted into the Inventor's Hall of Fame in 1975. The U.S. Postal Service honored him with a commemorative stamp in 1983. The Institute of Electrical Engineers established its Nikola Tesla Award in 1976 and is one of their most distinguished awards to receive.

Nikola Tesla was a most amazing man. He was the inventor of alternating current, x-rays, the radio, radar, hydroelectric energy, remote control, neon lighting, the modern electric motor, and wireless communication. To say Tesla would be entirely at home in our Twitter universe would be an understatement.

10 Things You Never Knew About Nikola Tesla

"He was the first to be thinking about the information revolution in the sense of delivering information for each individual user."

—W. Bernard Carlson

Did you know there is an auto company called Tesla? They offer state-of-the-art electric vehicles with all electric all-wheel drive and optional full self-driving hardware. You can harness the power of the sun with Tesla batteries too, which, combined with solar energy reduces your dependence on fossil fuels.

Tesla envisioned today's smartphone. All the way back in 1909, Tesla was quoted in The New York Times as saying, "It will only be necessary to carry an inexpensive instrument not bigger than a watch, which will enable its bearer to hear anywhere on sea or land for distances of thousands of miles. One may listen or transmit speech or song to the uttermost parts of the world. In the same way, any kind of picture, drawing, or print can be transferred from one place to another. It will be possible to operate millions of such instruments from a single station." Truly remarkable.

Tesla rarely slept. He claimed only to sleep two hours every night. Tesla could spend two or more days in his laboratory without sleeping at all. The most he would do is take the occasional short nap, to recharge his batteries, so he said.

Many of Tesla's inventions still remain classified. People have requested some of them via the Freedom of Information Act, and have received them, although they are highly censored. Conspiracies about what Tesla might have been working on later in his life have become popular conversation over the years.

Tesla had a great aversion to pearls. If a woman was wearing pearls, he would not speak with her. One day his secretary showed up for work wearing pearls, and he sent her home for the day. No one knows why he hated pearls, only that his mannerisms were very particular. He did seem to border on the obsessive-compulsive state of mind; every photograph ever taken of Tesla only shows his good side.

Tesla was an environmentalist. He worried that people all over the planet were too quickly consuming the Earth's resources. He did research on using natural energy from the ground and the sky. He believed this energy would be far better than the fossil fuel energy becoming so prevalent the world over. Tesla created artificial lightning in his lab.

Tesla's inventions went far beyond just everything electrical. His over 700 inventions included wireless connection and communication, x-rays, helicopters, torpedoes, turbine engines, and neon lights.

Tesla had a photographic memory. He read many, many books, and could memorize entire books. He also spoke eight languages, Serbo-Croatian, Czech, English, French, German, Hungarian, Italian and Latin. He also suffered from blinding flashes of light, which would lead him to visions of words or ideas that he had been working on. He was able to visualize a project in intricate detail in his mind before ever putting it down on paper. Many times he never drew any diagrams; his inventions were taken from his visions only.

Tesla became a good friend of the author Mark Twain. They spent a lot of time together in his lab and elsewhere. One of Tesla's devices was called a high-frequency oscillator, and it could shake a building rather violently. Twain was in attendance at one of Tesla's oscillator demonstrations and became so scared; he had to run to the bathroom.

Lastly, Tesla was born during a lightning storm. It was at the moment of his birth that the midwife wrung her hands and declared to his family that this was a bad omen. She told them "this child will be a child of darkness." Tesla's mother immediately replied, "No, he will be a child of light."

Conclusion

What is genius? Is it living up to your unique innate abilities? Hardly. Is there a "genius code" we should be on the lookout for? Could be. Why is it that some people seem to catch all the accolades that go along with being famous in what they do, while others seem never to emerge from behind the curtain?

Are you and I destined to a life of mediocrity? Or is there something more that goes hand in hand with what we have been given and whom we say we are? That something is imagination.

Nikola Tesla had it. All his life, Tesla let his imagination lead the way. It became his library, where he returned over and over to visit his blueprints; everything from alternating current to an electrical tower. Tesla was a true visionary.

That is why in his lifetime, he never amounted to much. He was awarded a few medals and honors, but the highest accolades and vast wealth would pass him by. Choosing to live alone, he died alone, but he never felt alone.

So the next time you watch that Frankenstein movie and see Dr. Frankenstein surrounded by his bolts of lightning and swirling coils aflame as his monster ascends to the open ceiling, think about Nikola Tesla. Sitting in his laboratory while massive bolts of electrical current ran from one side of the room to the other, Tesla's massive coil snuffed out the power as it went flying in all its electrical madness during his experiments. There he sat, underneath it all, with notebook and pen in hand, oblivious to all that was going on over his head.

Tesla really was a man out of time. He was perfect for the time he lived in, though, as what he invented would be our saving grace in the years he knew were coming.

For anyone out there who considers himself or herself to be a Tesla geek, there is always July 10th to look forward to. That is Nikola Tesla Day when you can be your most creative, obsessive, tinkering, imaginative self. And no one will question why.

When you use your smartphone or turn on the lights at home, know that that electrical current is still going strong. Tesla lived through the difficulties of his life to make all of our lives less difficult - at least when it comes to holding the whole world in our hands.

Made in the USA
Columbia, SC
11 January 2018